HEINEMANN STATE STUDIES

Uniquely North Dakota

Jim Redmond and D. J. Ross

Heinemann Library
Chicago, Illinois

© 2004 Heinemann Library
a division of Reed Elsevier Inc.
Chicago, Illinois

Customer Service 888-454-2279

Visit our website at www.heinemannlibrary.com

All rights reserved. No part of this publication may be reproduced or transmitted in any form or by any means, electronic or mechanical, including photocopying, recording, taping, or any information storage and retrieval system, without permission in writing from the publisher.

Designed by Heinemann Library
Printed in China by WKT Company Limited.

08 07 06 05 04
10 9 8 7 6 5 4 3 2 1

Library of Congress Cataloging-in-Publication Data

Redmond, Jim.
  Uniquely North Dakota / Jim Redmond.
    p. cm.—(Heinemann state studies)
  Includes index.
  ISBN 1-4034-4657-1 (hc library binding)—
  ISBN 1-4034-4726-8 (pb)
  1. North Dakota—Juvenile literature. I. Title.
  II. Series.
  F636.3.R44 2004
  978.4—dc22

2004002771

Cover Pictures

Top (left to right) wheat farm, Teddy Roosevelt in the Badlands, North Dakota state flag, Native Americans on reservation
Main Badlands

Acknowledgments
Development and photo research by
BOOK BUILDERS LLC

The author and publishers are grateful to the following for permission to reproduce copyrighted material:

Cover photographs by (top, L-R): Andre Jenny/Alamy; Popperfoto/Alamy; Joe Sohm/Alamy; Jim Richardson/Corbis; (main) Corbis.

Title page (L-R): Dawn Charging/North Dakota Tourism; Clayton Wolt/North Dakota Tourism; Jason Lindsey; Alamy; Contents page: North Dakota Tourism; p. 4, 35 Andre Jenny/Alamy; p. 5 Courtesy Greater Grand Forks Convention and Visitors Bureau; p. 6, 40 Jason Lindsey/Alamy; p. 7, 13T, 13B, 14T, 18, 30, 38, 41, 42, 44 North Dakota Tourism; p. 8, 39, 45 maps by IMA for BOOK BUILDERS LLC; p. 9T Pat Hertz/North Dakota Tourism; p. 9B Tom Bean/North Dakota Tourism; p. 10 Mick Erickson/USFWS; p. 11T Joe Sohm/Alamy; p. 11B, 15T, 15B, 20B, 37 Historical Society of North Dakota; p. 14B Dominique Braud/AnimalsAnimals; p. 16 Jim Richardson/Corbis; p. 20T, 22T Hulton Getty; p. 21 Courtesy Bantam Books/John Hamilton/Globe Photos; p. 22 Courtesy Harper Perennial; p. 23 Corbis; p. 24T Popperfoto/Alamy; p. 24B Bruce M. Kaye/North Dakota Tourism; p. 26 Clayton Wolt/North Dakota Tourism; p.28 Dawn Charging/North Dakota Tourism; p. 29 Courtesy Norsk Hostfest Association; p. 31 B. Minton/Heinemann Library; p. 32 R. Capozzelli/Heinemann Library; p. 33 Christine Osborne/Alamy; p. 34T, 34B Courtesy University of North Dakota Athletic Dept.; p. 43 Chuck Haney/North Dakota Tourism.

Special thanks to Dr. Gregory S. Camp of the State Historical Society of North Dakota for his expert comments in the preparation of this book.

Every effort has been made to contact copyright holders of any material reproduced in this book. Any omissions will be rectified in subsequent printings if notice is given to the publisher.

Some words are shown in bold, **like this.** You can find out what they mean by looking in the glossary.

Contents

Uniquely North Dakota 4
North Dakota's Geography and Climate . . . 6
Famous Firsts 9
North Dakota's State Symbols 11
North Dakota's History and People 16
The Badlands 23
North Dakota's State Government 25
North Dakota's Culture 28
North Dakota's Food 30
North Dakota's Folklore and Legends 32
North Dakota's Sports Teams 34
North Dakota's Businesses and Products .36
Attractions and Landmarks 38
Map of North Dakota 45
Glossary 46
More Books to Read 47
Index 48
About the Authors 48

Uniquely North Dakota

Unique means one of a kind. North Dakota is unique in many ways. The state is the geographic center of North America and the home of Minot Air Force Base, one of the most important military bases in the country. North Dakota also grows more sunflowers than any other state, and it is home to the largest buffalo monument in the world.

ORIGIN OF THE STATE'S NAME

The word *dakota* means "friend" and comes from the language of the Lakota people, a tribe **native** to the region.

MAJOR CITIES

North Dakota has a population of about 640,000, which is about the same population as Memphis, Tennessee. Because so few people live in North Dakota, its cities are small. Not one has more than 100,000 people.

Founded in 1871, Fargo also grew as a result of the railroad industry. The city began as a tent town where

Fargo was named for William G. Fargo of the Wells-Fargo Express Company, which delivered money and goods across the country in the 1800s.

Northern Pacific Railroad engineers lived in the tents and planned the growth of the railway. The city lies in the eastern part of the state on the Red River. It has a population of about 90,000 people and is the largest city in North Dakota.

Bismarck, the capital, is located near the center of the state. In 1868 the Great Northern Railroad built Bismarck to attract settlers to work the railroad. It served as a connecting point between railways traveling east and west, and it became known as "the gateway to the West." Today, the city has a population of about 55,000 people.

North of Fargo on the Red River lies Grand Forks, a city with about 50,000 residents. Fur traders settled the area in the 1790s. In 1881, when Grand Forks officially became a city, it was a trading center for wheat, potatoes, and sugar beets. In 1997 a flood severely damaged the city. Melting winter snow combined with an ice storm caused the Red River to overflow. Almost every house in Grand Forks had to be evacuated.

The Grand Forks Visitor's Center welcomes people who came to the Alerus Center for concerts and Engelstad Arena for hockey.

North Dakota's Geography and Climate

North Dakota is about 335 miles wide and 210 miles long and is a rectangular shape. Minnesota borders it to the east, Canada to the north, Montana to the west, and South Dakota to the south. Three geographical regions cover the state: the Red River Valley, the Drift Prairie, and the Great Plains.

Land

The Red River Valley, in the eastern part of the state, borders Minnesota. **Glaciers** formed this region. **Silt** deposited by the glaciers makes this some of the best farmland in the world. The Red River Valley has been called "the breadbasket of the world," because so much wheat

The flat land and good soil of the Great Plains are ideal for growing wheat.

Devil's Lake

Devil's Lake, the largest natural body of water in North Dakota, keeps growing, even though no streams or springs flow into the lake. Rainwater and melting snow drain into the lake through coulees, which are natural depressions in the land that lead to the lake. In the 1930s, during a long period of dryness, the lake covered only 75 acres. Now it covers more than 100,000 acres.

is grown there. The Red River Valley's elevation is only about 800 feet above sea level.

To the west of the Red River Valley, the Drift Prairie gradually emerges. Glaciers also formed the Drift Prairie. This area has many rolling **plains** and **sloughs,** where thousands of ducks and geese nest each year.

The Great Plains cover the western half of the state. Water, wind, and underground fires formed much of this area. Millions of years ago, lightning struck the ground, causing **lignite coal** to burn under the ground's surface. The coal baked until it became hard as brick. Wind and rain eroded the soil until the baked coal rose to the surface. The elevation in the Great Plains reaches as high 3,506 feet above sea level at White Butte.

CLIMATE AND PRECIPITATION

North Dakota has a subhumid continental **climate.** This type of climate has hot summers and cold winters. The record high in summer is 121°F, and the record low in winter is −60°F. Average temperatures range from 70°F in July down to 10°F in January.

The wind blows freely across the plains of North Dakota. **Chinook winds** blow warm air across the western part of the state. This causes the western part of the state to be an average of 10°F warmer than the eastern part. These winds also can cause huge jumps in temperature. For example, on February 21, 1918, a Chinook wind caused the temperature at Granville to rise from 33°F below zero in the morning to 50°F degrees above zero in the afternoon.

Most precipitation falls in the spring and early summer, but more rain falls in the eastern part of the state than in the western part. North Dakota averages from thirteen inches of precipitation in the northwest to twenty inches in the southeast. Although a northern state, North Dakota averages less than 38 inches of snow per year. This amount is less than states such as New York, Michigan, and Pennsylvania receive, some of which average more than 100 inches per year. However, the state can experience heavy snows. For example, in early January 1989, Fargo was struck by a three-day snowstorm during which 24.4 inches of snow fell on the city.

This climagraph shows the temperature and precipitation in Bismarck.

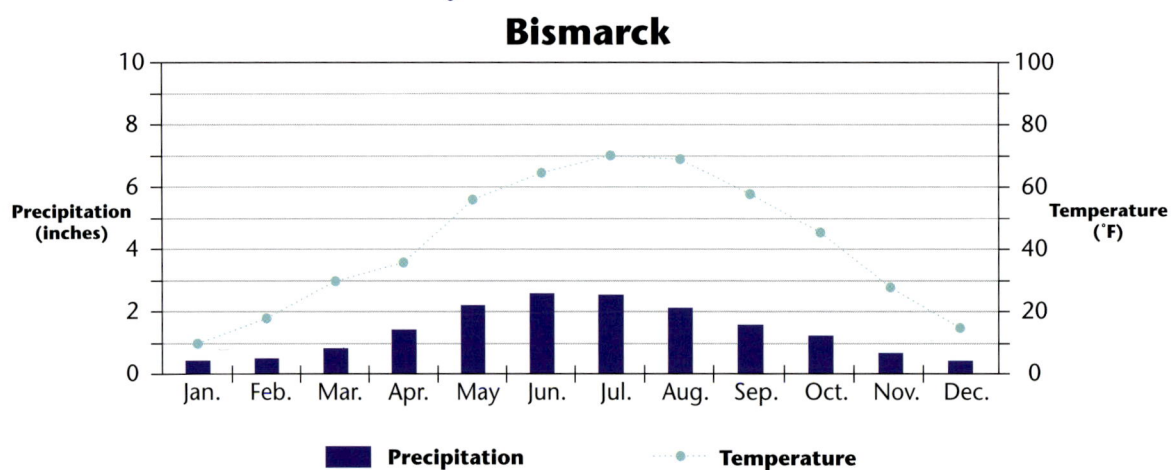

Famous Firsts

The town of Rugby is the geographical center of North America—exactly in the middle of the continent. A rock **obelisk** about 21 feet tall marks the location.

Started during the energy crisis of the 1970s, the Dakota Gasification Company in Beulah is the nation's only **synthetic** natural gas producer. The company pumps oxygen and steam into burning **lignite coal** to make natural gas. The natural gas is then pumped through pipelines to provide energy to many eastern states.

This monument was completed in 1932.

The world's largest buffalo monument stands at Frontier Village in Jamestown. The structure is 26 feet high and 46 feet long, weighs 60 tons, and looks like a giant buffalo. Frontier Village has its own herd of buffalo. Within this herd is a white buffalo named White Cloud, one of the rarest animals on Earth.

*One out of a billion buffalo are **albino.***

Built in 1909, the North Dakota State University research experiment station in Hettinger was one of the first places to study farm-related plants and animals. Scientists in one part of the research station study sheep to find ways to make them healthier and grow more quickly. The center is the largest state-owned sheep research center in the United States.

North Dakota has 60 wildlife **refuges,** more than any other state. Many of these refuges are **wetlands** and provide shelter for ducks, geese, and swans. Whooping cranes stop in North Dakota twice each year on their last natural **flyway.** Each year they fly from the Gulf of Mexico to Alberta, Canada, and back again. One of the world's largest nesting colonies of pelicans makes its home at Chase Lake, a wildlife refuge covering 5.5 million acres.

The North Dakota Mill and Elevator Association is the only state-owned flour mill in the United States. It helps North Dakota wheat farmers get a fair price for their product. It produces many different kinds of flour, such as all-purpose, bread, and whole wheat.

Bank of North Dakota

The Bank of North Dakota, located in Bismarck, is the only state-owned bank in the nation. The North Dakota **legislature** established the bank in 1919. During the early 1900s, North Dakota's economy was based on farming. At that time serious economic problems hurt farmers and they wanted the state to help them. Thus, the state legislature established the Bank of North Dakota, which was to encourage and promote agriculture, commerce, and industry in the state.

Chase Lake National Wildlife Refuge is home to more than one-third of all white pelicans in North America.

North Dakota's State Symbols

North Dakota adopted its state flag on January 21, 1911.

NORTH DAKOTA STATE FLAG

The bald eagle on North Dakota's state flag represents the United States. The olive branch it carries in its claws represents peace, and the arrows represent strength. A shield on the eagle's breast has thirteen stripes, which represent the first thirteen states. A fan-shaped design above the eagle represents a new nation being born.

NORTH DAKOTA STATE SEAL

The state seal symbolizes North Dakota's Native American heritage and the agricultural products grown in the state. The North Dakota Great Seal is the state's only symbol that is protected by state law. It cannot be reproduced or changed in any way or used in advertising.

The North Dakota Great Seal was adopted in 1889, the year it became a state.

STATE MOTTO: "LIBERTY AND UNION NOW AND FOREVER, ONE AND INSEPARABLE"

The motto of North Dakota is "Liberty and Union Now and Forever, One and Inseparable." It is a quote from a famous speech by Senator Daniel Webster of Massachusetts. The motto of the Dakota Territory was "Liberty and Union, One and Inseparable, Now and Forever." Dr.

An Unofficial Nickname

In the 1960s and 1970s North Dakota called itself the Roughrider State to promote tourism. "Roughriders" was the nickname of the First U.S. Cavalry that Theodore Roosevelt led during the **Spanish–American War** (1898). The Roughriders charged up San Juan Hill in Cuba, helping that country win independence from Spain. Theodore Roosevelt, who once lived in North Dakota, went on to become governor of New York and then president of the United States.

Joseph Ward of Yankton (now South Dakota), who was quoting Webster, suggested it. However, the motto of the territory had two of the phrases reversed. When North Dakota became a state in 1889, the error was corrected.

State Nickname: Peace Garden State

The official nickname for North Dakota is the Peace Garden State. The name comes from the International Peace

"North Dakota Hymn"

North Dakota, North Dakota,
With thy prairies wide and free,
All thy sons and daughters love thee,
Fairest state from sea to sea;
North Dakota, North Dakota,
Here we pledge ourselves to thee.

Hear thy loyal children singing,
Songs of happiness and praise,
Far and long the echoes ringing,
Through the vastness of thy ways;
North Dakota, North Dakota,
We will serve thee all our days.

Onward, onward, onward going,
Light of courage in thine eyes,
Sweet the winds above thee blowing,
Green thy fields and fair thy skies;
North Dakota, North Dakota,
Brave the soul that in thee lies.

God of freedom, all victorious,
Give us Souls serene and strong,
Strength to make the future glorious,
Keep the echo of our song;
North Dakota, North Dakota,
In our hearts forever long.

Garden, which is located in North Dakota and in the Canadian province of Manitoba. Built in 1932, the garden honors the friendship between the United States and Canada. It is the only park jointly owned by two countries.

State Tree: American Elm

North Dakota adopted the American elm as its state tree in 1947. The elm is a common tree throughout the Midwest.

State Song: "North Dakota Hymn"

In 1926 the superintendent of public instruction, Minnie J. Nielson, asked Bismarck poet James Foley to write the lyrics for a song about North Dakota. Foley created a poem to be sung to an Austrian hymn. The North Dakota Hymn was presented to the public in 1927.

State Flower: Wild Prairie Rose

The wild prairie rose is the state flower of North Dakota. It grows along roadsides, in pastures, and in meadows. The wild prairie rose has five bright pink petals that surround a yellow center.

State Bird: Western Meadowlark

Because the western meadowlark lives across the Great Plains, it was chosen as the state bird of North Dakota. The meadowlark has a yellow breast with a black bib over a mottled brown body.

The American elm can grow to more than 120 feet tall.

North Dakota adopted the western meadowlark as its state bird in 1947.

Northern pike can weigh more than twenty pounds.

State Fish: Northern Pike

North Dakota's state fish is the northern pike. These large fish are plentiful in North Dakota waters, and people come from all over the United States to catch them. Northern pike can grow up to four feet long and live between 10 and 26 years.

Honorary State Equine: Nokota Horse

Nokota horses are a unique type of horse that once ran wild in the Badlands. Europeans first saw these wild horses during the late 1800s. Many people believe the Nokota horses are the last of Lakota Chief Sitting Bull's herd. In the mid-1900s the National Park Service tried to remove all these wild horses from the Badlands. Native Americans and others urged the North Dakota government to designate the Nokota horse the Honorary State Equine. The **legislature** did so in 1993. Today, conservation groups are working to establish a safe area where the Nokota horses can roam free and wild.

The Nokota horses are believed to be descended from Lakota Chief Sitting Bull's war ponies.

State Fossil: Teredo

The Teredo was a wormlike animal that dug into trees 60 to 80 million years ago in what is today North Dakota. The trees grew near swamps. Minerals from the swamps **petrified** the Teredo and the tree, turning them into fossils. The legislature made the Teredo the state fossil in 1967.

"The Flickertail March" gets its name from the flickertail squirrel, which is common in North Dakota.

STATE MARCH: "THE FLICKERTAIL MARCH"

In 1975 the North Dakota legislature hired James D. Ployhar to write a state march. He named it "Spirit of the Land," but another march had the same title, so he changed it to "The Flickertail March."

STATE DANCE: SQUARE DANCE

In 1995 the legislature named the square dance the state dance. It is the most popular folk dance in the United States. The dance, for four couples, is done within a square, with each couple forming a side. Traditionally, a fiddle, an accordion, a banjo, and a guitar play square dance music. A "caller" indicates the different steps the couples perform.

STATE GRASS: WESTERN WHEATGRASS

In 1977 the legislature chose western wheatgrass as the state grass because it once grew in all the state's counties. Before European settlers tilled the land for farming, western wheatgrass covered nearly all of North Dakota. The grass grows up to three feet tall.

Western wheatgrass adapts to many soil conditions.

North Dakota's History and People

The story of what is today North Dakota begins in prehistory—the time before events were written down. The earliest people were nomads who followed the animals they hunted for food and clothing.

NATIVE AMERICANS

In the years before the Europeans arrived, many Native American nations lived in the area. Among these nations were the Assiniboine, Ojibwe, Cree, Hidatsa, and Arikara. Others, such as the Lakota and Chippewa, followed the bison across the **plains.**

The Mandan settled in what is today North Dakota in the 1300s and lived in permanent **earth lodges** that measured up to 50 feet across. Mandan families slept on beds made of tanned animal hides stuffed with prairie grass. A fire pit inside the earthlodge provided heat and a place to cook food, which they grew in large gardens. The floors had holes dug in them to provide a storage place for corn, beans, and squash.

Lakota Native American culture is still very important in North Dakota.

The Lakota originally lived in wooded areas of what is now Minnesota, but many Lakota followed the bison west to present-day North Dakota. In the 1600s some Lakota tribes settled in the area.

Early Explorers

The first recorded European to explore North Dakota was Pierre La Vérendrye, from France. He came south from Canada in 1738, searching for a passage to the Pacific Ocean to expand the French fur trade.

More than a half century later, Alexander Henry Jr. established a fur-trading post at Pembina. The area was home to several Native American tribes, including the Ojibwe, Lakota, and Cree.

In 1803 President Thomas Jefferson purchased the Louisiana Territory from the French. Covering about 820,000 acres, this vast new land stretched west of the Mississippi River to the Rocky Mountains. It more than doubled the size of the United States. These new lands were a mystery to the people of the United States, because most of them lived within 50 miles of the Atlantic Ocean.

Jefferson hired Meriwether Lewis and William Clark to explore the new lands. The Lewis and Clark expedition had several goals. One was to find an easy water route to the Pacific Ocean. Another was to establish good terms with the **native** people so trade could expand west. Lewis and Clark also mapped out the territory.

In 1804 Lewis and Clark spent the winter near what is now Washburn. More than 4,500 Hidatsa lived in the area, which was more people than lived in the city of St. Louis, Missouri, or Washington, D.C. The Hidatsa befriended Lewis and Clark and helped them lead their voyage west.

Sacajawea

Sacajawea was a Shoshone who lived with the Hidatsa in what is today North Dakota. When Lewis and Clark reached this area, they hired Toussaint Charbonneau, Sacajawea's husband—and a French fur trader—as a guide. Sacajawea, who just had a baby, went with them. She carried her son, Jean-Baptiste, on her back from her village to the Pacific Ocean. On the journey she helped in many ways. She **bartered** with the Shoshone for horses and supplies. She gathered wild beans and artichokes for food. She saved Lewis and Clark's journals and medicine that had washed out of one of the canoes during a storm. Today, a twelve-foot-high bronze statue of Sacajawea and her son stands at the entrance to the North Dakota Heritage Center on the state capitol grounds in Bismarck.

American Settlement and Native American Wars

American pioneers began settling the area after the U.S. Congress organized the Dakota Territory in 1861. Immigrants poured into the territory to build the Northern Pacific Railroad in 1872 and 1873. New towns sprang up to serve the settlers, the track-laying crews, and other frontier citizens. Fargo and Bismarck, for example, both began as rough-and-tumble railroad towns.

Between 1879 and 1886 more than 100,000 people entered the territory. Many were family farmers, but some organized large, highly mechanized **bonanza farms.** Immigrants from Germany, Norway, Sweden, Russia, and Ukraine came to the Dakota Territory.

In the early 1860s Native Americans began fighting the European pioneers who tried to take over the area the

Native Americans had traditionally used for their hunting grounds. The U.S. government tried to force the Native Americans to live on reservations, instead of living on the open **plains.** The U.S. army searched the area for Native Americans who refused to move to reservations. Battles at Whitestone Hill (1863), at Killdeer Mountain (1864), and in the Badlands (1864) forced many **native** people onto reservations. In the 1870s the U.S. army began slaughtering the buffalo herds. In this way, the army hoped to remove the Native American's food supply. Small groups of Lakota resisted into the 1880s, but their old way of life on the plains was lost.

Statehood

As early as 1877 the settlers of the Dakota Territory began calling for statehood. On November 2, 1889, both North Dakota and South Dakota were admitted to the Union. After President Benjamin Harrison signed the official statehood documents, he mixed them up because he did not want to favor one state over the other. Because of alphabetical position, North Dakota is considered the 39th state and South Dakota the 40th state.

Famous People

Ivan Dmitre (1900–1968), artist. Born Levon West, his family lived throughout North Dakota when he was a child. He gained fame after one of his etchings, "The Spirit of St. Louis," was published. Soon, art collectors were paying high prices for his work. West then became interested in photography. His photographs also brought him fame. To keep his two careers separate, his used the name "Ivan Dmitre" with his photographs. Museums across the world have shown his work.

As a TV bandleader, Lawrence Welk led musicians through light, melodic waltzes and polkas with his catch prases, "Ah-one, ah-two" and "Wunnerful, wunnerful."

Lawrence Welk (1903–1992), bandleader. Born in Strasburg, Lawrence Welk was reared in a strict German family and did not learn to speak English until he was 21 years old. Welk entertained friends and neighbors with his accordion, playing at age 13. In 1955 the *Lawrence Welk Show* was broadcast on television. For the next 26 years, Welk's show of popular, easy-listening music entertained families across the country. Reruns of Welk's shows are still popular.

Ronald N. Davies (1904–1996), federal **jurist.** Ronald N. Davies attended high school in Grand Forks and college at the University of North Dakota. In 1932 he was elected a judge in Grand Forks and was later appointed a federal district court judge. In 1957 Davies ordered the **integration** of Central High School at Little Rock, Arkansas. His order enforced rulings of the U.S. Supreme Court.

Era Bell Thompson (1905–1986), journalist. Era Bell Thompson grew up in North Dakota and attended the University of North Dakota. She wrote several books and became an editor for *Ebony* magazine, the world's largest African American–owned magazine.

Casper Oimoen was captain of the U.S. Olympic ski team in 1936.

Casper Oimoen (1906–1995), skier. Casper Oimoen was born in Norway but grew up in Minot. He won more than 400 medals and trophies. In 1930 he won the Eastern, Central, and National Championships in ski jumping.

Edward K. Thompson (1907–1996), editor. Edward K. Thompson lived much of his life in North Dakota, where he edited a newspa-

per in Fargo. Thompson edited *Life* magazine for more than twenty years, then founded *Smithsonian,* the magazine of the Smithsonian Institution in Washington, D.C.

Louis L'Amour (1908–1988), writer. Born Louis Dearborn LaMoore in Jamestown, L'Amour's books centered on the Wild West. As a boy, he watched the last remaining cowhands come through town and he dreamed of the old west. During the 1930s and 1940s L'Amour published hundreds of magazine stories. In 1953 he wrote his first novel, *Hondo.* His novels became popular and many of his books were made into movies. L'Amour wrote more than 100 novels, 65 television scripts, and 30 movie scripts.

Millions of copies of Louis L'Amour's books have been sold.

Dr. Leon O. Jacobson (1911–1992), medical researcher. Leon Jacobson grew up in North Dakota and taught all eight grades in a two-room schoolhouse. Later, he became a leader in **chemotherapy** research. Chemotherapy is a treatment used to fight cancer.

Eric Severeid (1912–1992), newscaster. Born in Velva, Eric Severeid became a journalist and then a national radio correspondent during **World War II** (1939–1945). After the war, he worked as a television newsman and reported on presidential elections.

Anne Carlsen (1915–2002), educator, activist. Born in Wisconsin without fully developed arms or legs, Anne Carlsen learned to swim and play baseball and other games. After attending college, Carlsen took a job at the Good Samaritan School for Crippled Children in Fargo. Carlsen continued her work at the school, which moved to Jamestown, and eventually became the prin-

Roger Maris' #9 jersey has been retired in the New York Yankees' Monument Park.

Louise Erdich is a member of the Turtle Mountain Band of Ojibwe.

cipal. Throughout her life, she championed the causes for handicapped people. In 1980 the name of the school was changed to the Anne Carlsen Center.

Roger Maris (1934–1985), baseball player. Born in Fargo, Roger Maris excelled in both baseball and football as a high school athlete. After high school, Maris became a legendary outfielder for the New York Yankees. In 1961, he broke Babe Ruth's single-season home run record by hitting 61. The record stood for 37 years. Maris won two Most Valuable Player awards and went to seven World Series.

Phil D. Jackson (1945–), basketball coach. Phil Jackson has led his current team, the Los Angeles Lakers, to National Basketball Association titles in 2000, 2001, and 2002. Before that, he coached the Chicago Bulls to six titles from 1991 to 1993 and 1996 to 1998. His love for the game started in Williston, where he played on the high school team.

Louise Erdrich (1954–), author. Louise Erdrich was born in Minnesota but grew up in Wahpeton, where her parents taught at Bureau of Indian Affairs schools. Erdrich writes books about Native American life. She won the National Book Critics Circle Award in 1984 for her novel *Love Medicine*.

The Badlands

The Badlands are an area of North Dakota where severe **erosion** has caused gullies and ridges to form. The ridges are made from different rock types that create beautiful formations.

Geography of the Badlands

About 500,000 years ago, underground fires and erosion helped shape the Badlands of western North Dakota. The fires started when lightning struck the ground and lit buried coal beds on fire. These fires baked the clay and dirt over the coal into reddish rocks. Hard rains washed away the loose dirt around the rocks, leaving red ridges and **buttes,** or hills. Because the tops are flat as a table, buttes also are referred to as tablelands.

Along with the reddish rocks, blue-gray clay colors the Badlands. The clay formed from large amounts of volcanic ash that blew over the area millions of years ago.

Erosion formed much of the Badlands.

During this same period the Badlands were swampy and filled with forests. When the trees died they sank into the water. Some trees decayed into the coal that is under the ground. Other trees were **petrified** by minerals in the water. Petrified trees are found throughout the Badlands.

Many plants and animals live in the Badlands, even though the **climate** is very dry. An average of only fifteen inches of rain falls each year. Wildflowers bloom purple, blue, and yellow. Lush grasses grow on the tablelands, and trees grow along the rivers. Mule deer, coyotes, wild horses, and bison all call the badlands home.

THEODORE ROOSEVELT IN THE BADLANDS

When **Theodore Roosevelt** was 24 years old, he came from New York City to the Badlands in search of adventure. He found it ten days into his trip when he hunted bison. Roosevelt came to love the area so much that he bought two cattle ranches there, the Maltese Cross and the Elkhorn. From 1883 to 1892 Roosevelt lived in the Badlands as a cowboy. He found this life refreshing, and years later he wrote, "I would not have been President, had it not been for my experience in North Dakota."

THEODORE ROOSEVELT NATIONAL PARK

Theodore Roosevelt National Park is the only national park named after a person. It offers a unique view of old-time western life, and the cabin where Theodore Roosevelt lived as he ranched stands near the Little Missouri River. Today, as back then, bison and wild horses run free over the blue-gray earth.

Theodore Roosevelt was the 26th president of the United States.

About 100 wild horses still roam Theodore Roosevelt National Park.

North Dakota's State Government

North Dakota's government is based in Bismarck, the capital. The state is governed by a constitution, which is a plan of government approved by the state's people. North Dakota is the only state that does not require voters to register to vote.

The constitution that governs North Dakota today went into effect at statehood in 1889. It promises many freedoms for North Dakota's people, including freedom of

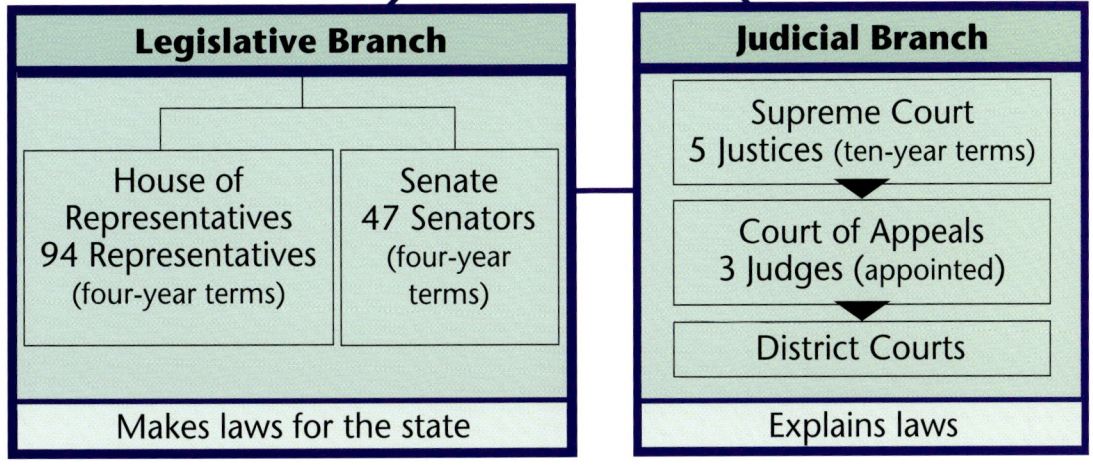

religion, speech, and the press. These basic rights are based on those listed in the U.S. Constitution.

North Dakota's government is similar to the federal government in Washington, D.C. Like the federal government, North Dakota's government is made up of three branches—the legislative, the executive, and the judicial.

The Legislative Branch

North Dakota's **legislature,** known as the legislative assembly, makes the state's laws. It consists of two houses—the Senate and the House of Representatives. As of 2003, the state is divided into 47 districts. Each district elects one senator and two representatives.

A bill, or proposed law, may start in either house of the legislature. When a majority, or more than half, of the members of both houses, has approved a bill, it is sent to the governor. If the governor signs the bill, it becomes a law. If the governor vetoes, or rejects, the bill, it becomes law only if a majority of the legislature votes to override the veto.

North Dakota's capitol was completed in 1934 and is more than 240 feet tall.

THE EXECUTIVE BRANCH

The executive branch enforces the state's laws and runs the state from day to day. The governor, who is elected to a four-year term, is the head of this branch.

Voters also elect other officials in the executive branch to four-year terms. These officials include the lieutenant governor, secretary of state, the attorney general, and the treasurer.

THE JUDICIAL BRANCH

The district courts are the main courts in North Dakota. They may hear all types of cases, including **criminal** and **civil** cases. The district courts also serve as the juvenile courts in the state. Thus, the district courts hear all cases involving children and young people. The state is divided into seven judicial districts, each with a presiding judge. District judges are elected every six years in a **nonpartisan** election.

The court of appeals hears only the cases assigned to it by the state Supreme Court. In some years, the Supreme Court assigns no cases to the court of appeals. Three judges, chosen from among active and retired judges and attorneys, serve on the court of appeals.

The Supreme Court is the highest court in the state. Its five justices are elected in nonpartisan elections for ten-year terms. The Supreme Court justices and the judges of the district courts select one member of the Supreme Court as the chief justice, for a term of five years. The Supreme Court has two major types of tasks—judging and administering. In its judging function, the Supreme Court serves as an appellate court. It hears appeals from the district courts and the court of appeals. The Supreme Court also oversees the operation of all the state courts.

North Dakota's Culture

Much of North Dakota's culture centers around the legacy of its frontier days. People celebrate the lifestyles of settlers and Native Americans. The population boom of the late 1800s and early 1900s brought many different ethnic groups to the area, which further enriched its culture.

Legacy of the Frontier

Rodeos in North Dakota help to celebrate the western history of the state. Almost 50 local and regional rodeos attract hundreds of cowhands to the state.

The United Tribes International Powwow

Drums beat and Native Americans dance in brightly colored feathers and beads. More than 70 Native American tribes participate in events at the United Tribes International **Powwow** in Bismarck each September. The powwow teaches many aspects of Native American culture, including how to make beads, quilts, leather, pottery, and jewelry.

The Norsk Hostfest features a variety of entertainers, including the Norwegian Sweater Dancers and the Norsk Hostfest Troll.

The Cowboy Poetry Gathering in Medora is the oldest ongoing regional cowboy poetry gathering in the country. Since 1986 poets have gathered from dozens of states to read poems that reflect and preserve cowboy culture.

Down-Home Dakota Culture and Diversity

The Norsk Hostfest, celebrated in Minot every October, is the largest Scandinavian festival in North America. People come to honor the traditions of Norway, Sweden, Denmark, Iceland, and Finland. Some traditional displays include hand-carved chairs, knit wool sweaters, and woven tablecloths. People also come to eat traditional food such as **lutefisk,** a type of fish, and **lefse,** a type of potato bread.

The North Dakota State Fair is the largest annual event in the state, with more than 200,000 people attending each year. Held every July in Minot, the fair highlights the state's food, flowers, agriculture, and livestock. Carnival rides offer excitement, and well-known singers perform on stage. Unique events include the Paul Bunyan Lumberjack Show, which features logrolling, chain sawing, and axe throwing.

North Dakota's Food

Most of the food eaten in North Dakota is grown in the state. Local farms provide people with a variety of foods.

One beef animal produces enough beef to make 1,800 quarter-pound hamburgers.

Beef

Cattle ranches have been a large part of North Dakota's economy since the 1880s and beef is an important food in the state. There are two million beef cattle in North Dakota, about three cows for every one person.

Sunflowers

Sunflowers grow between five and ten feet high. Each flower contains about 1,000 seeds. Two types of sunflowers grow in North Dakota. The black sunflower produces seeds that contain up to 44 percent oil. The oil gets taken out of the seed and is used for cooking. The striped sunflower's seeds are not oily. People eat these types of seeds.

Wheat and Grains

More than one-fourth of the land in North Dakota grows wheat. Wheat and grains are used to make many kinds of food. For example, durum wheat is used to make pasta and hard red spring wheat is used to make bread.

Dakota Bread

Dakota bread uses many ingredients from the state. This recipe is from former governor Edward T. Schafer. **Remember to have an adult help you.**

1 package active dry yeast
1/2 cup warm water (105 to 110°F)
2 tablespoons sunflower oil
1 egg
1/2 cup cottage cheese
1/4 cup honey
1 teaspoon salt
2 to 2-1/2 cups bread flour
1/2 cup whole wheat flour
1/4 cup wheat germ
1/4 cup rye flour
1/4 cup rolled oats
cornmeal

Sprinkle yeast in warm water; stir to dissolve. In a large bowl, mix sunflower oil, egg, cottage cheese, honey, and salt. Add dissolved yeast and two cups bread flour, beating until flour is moistened. Gradually stir in whole wheat flour, wheat germ, rye flour, and oats, plus enough bread flour to make a soft dough.

On a floured surface, knead dough for about ten minutes or until dough is smooth and elastic. Place dough in a greased bowl; cover loosely with oiled plastic wrap. Let rise in warm place until doubled in size, about 30 minutes.

Punch down dough. Shape into one round loaf. Place into a greased pie pan sprinkled with cornmeal. Cover with oiled plastic wrap and let rise until doubled in size (about one hour).

Brush with egg white and sprinkle with wheat germ, sunflower kernels, or oatmeal. Bake at 350 degrees for 35 to 40 minutes. Remove from pie pan and cool on a wire rack. Yield: one loaf (two pounds).

Note: If too dark, cover loosely with foil the last 10 to 15 minutes of baking.

North Dakota's Folklore and Legends

Some North Dakota legends have to do with settlers and farming, while others reflect Native American thoughts and ideas. In Lakota folklore, animals often represent people or explain history.

Wrong Side Up

Many years ago an elderly man watched a pioneer as he prepared to plant wheat by plowing the prairie grass. When the pioneer stopped, the man walked up to him, picked up a clod of grass that had been turned over by the plow, and said, "Wrong side up."

The man was referring to the millions of acres of rich soil in North Dakota that blew away with the wind because the pioneers had turned the prairie grass the "wrong side up."

SHEEPHERDER'S MONUMENTS

Piles of rock on White Butte, North Dakota's highest point, are knows as **rock johnnies** or sheepherders' monuments. According to legend, sheepherders piled rocks there to pass the time while they tended their flocks.

DREAM CATCHERS

When the world was young, an old Lakota spiritual leader sat on a mountain and had a vision. In his vision Iktomi, the great teacher of wisdom, appeared in the form of a spider. Iktomi took the old Lakota's willow hoop, which had feathers, horsehair, and beads on it, and began to spin a web. As he spun, Iktomi spoke of the cycle of life—how children grow to adulthood, then grow old and need to be taken care of again, as if they were children. He spoke of harmony and how both good and bad things influence life. When Iktomi finished spinning his web, a hole remained in the center. He told the old Lakota, "If you believe in the Great Spirit, the web will catch your good dreams, and the bad ones will go through the hole."

Lakota Dream Catchers are still made and used today.

North Dakota's Sports Teams

North Dakota has no major league sports teams. Instead, sports fans cheer college teams.

In 1999 the Fighting Sioux became the second team ever to win three straight Western Collegiate Hockey Association titles.

College Sports

The North Dakota Fighting Sioux hockey team is the only National Collegiate Athletic Association (NCAA) Division I sports program in the state. The team has a rich and successful history. They have won seven NCAA national championships, the first in 1959 and the most recent in 2000.

The women's cross-country team at the University of North Dakota appeared in the NCAA National Cross-Country meet eight times between 1991 and 2002. In 2000 they finished second in

The Fighting Sioux's women's cross country team finished second in the 2000 national meet.

The Fargodome opened in 1992. It hosts North Dakota State's athletic events.

the national meet, the highest finish in school history. That year the coach, Dick Clay, won national coach of the year honors.

The North Dakota State Bison play in the North Central Conference of college athletics. The conference is made up of Division II schools from North Dakota, Minnesota, Nebraska, South Dakota, and Colorado. Division II schools are generally smaller than Division I schools.

Led by coach Amy Ruley, a Fargo native, the North Dakota State women's basketball team has achieved great success during Ruley's 24-year tenure. She has coached the team to five NCAA Division II national titles and seventeen playoff appearances.

The women's softball team at North Dakota State won the NCAA Division II national championship in 2000. With a record of 68-10, the team set a Division II record for the most wins in a season. The Bison softball team reached the NCAA tournament four times in a row from 1997 to 2001.

North Dakota's Businesses and Products

In North Dakota many people work in farm-related jobs, in the coal-mining industry, or in the oil business. Other people work at the Minot Air Force Base.

Agriculture

Agriculture is North Dakota's number one industry, with one out of four people working in farm-related jobs. Farms and ranches make up 90 percent of North Dakota's land and would cover 12 million city blocks. Farmers and ranchers produce enough beef to make 2 billion hamburgers, enough wheat to make bread for 108 billion sandwiches, and enough durum wheat for 93 pounds of pasta for every American.

Agriculture is a $3 billion industry that provides 37 percent of the state's economy.

North Dakota is one of the top three **organic farming** states in the nation. Organic farmers do not spray crops with chemicals to kill weeds and insects. Instead, they use natural ways to enrich the soil and to stop insect damage.

North Dakota also produces more crops such as flaxseed, pinto beans, and sunflowers than any other state.

Minot Air Force Base

Minot Air Force base was built during the Cold War (1945–1991), a time of great tension between the United States and the former Soviet Union. Each nation viewed the other as a threat. The U.S. government built Minot Air Force base to prevent a Soviet attack from the north. Thousands of missiles, which are housed in missile silos, are connected to an underground launch control center. The Minuteman III missile has a 6,000-mile range and travels at 15,000 miles per hour. The base is also home to one of two B-52H Stratofortress bomber bases in the nation. The base adds more than $250 million to the state each year.

Oil and Coal

Western North Dakota contains an estimated 351 billion tons of **lignite coal** that can be mined, the largest deposit known in the world. Most of the coal is burned to provide electricity. North Dakota ranks ninth nationally in oil production. About 33 million barrels of oil are produced each year.

Oil was discovered in North Dakota in 1951.

Attractions and Landmarks

Many attractions and landmarks celebrate the history of Native Americans and European settlers. Preserved landmarks such as Native American villages show what life was like before European settlers arrived.

MENOKEN VILLAGE SITE

Native Americans first lived at the Menoken Village site, located near Menoken, about 900 years ago. Many of the **earth lodges** they lived in still stand. The site contains **artifacts** from before the Mandan Native Americans settled there, and it may be the village that the La Vérendrye expedition found in 1738. The Menoken Village Site is listed on the National Register of Historic Places.

WRITING ROCK STATE HISTORIC SITE

Located near Grenora, Writing Rock State Historic Site is famous for its petroglyphs, or rock writings. Prehistoric

Menoken lived in earth lodges.

Native Americans of the Great Plains probably drew the images. The drawings show a thunderbird, a fabled figure sacred to the early Plains peoples. Today, many **native** groups believe the site is sacred.

The Writing Rock site, open from May 15 until September 15, was acquired by North Dakota in 1936 and a protective shelter over the rocks was built in 1956.

Dakota Dinosaur Museum

The Dakota Dinosaur Museum in Dickinson houses eleven full-scale dinosaurs inside and three full-scale

Places to see in North Dakota

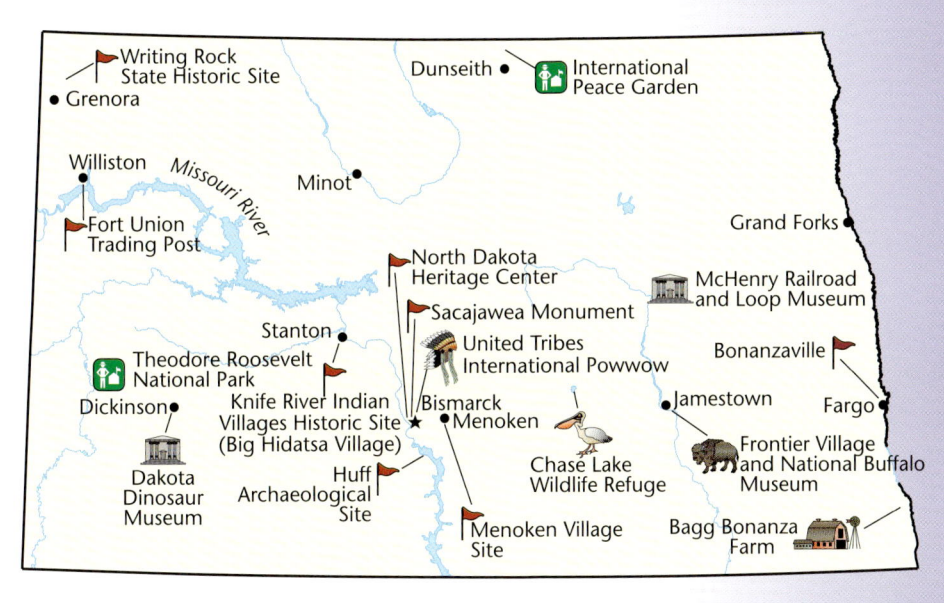

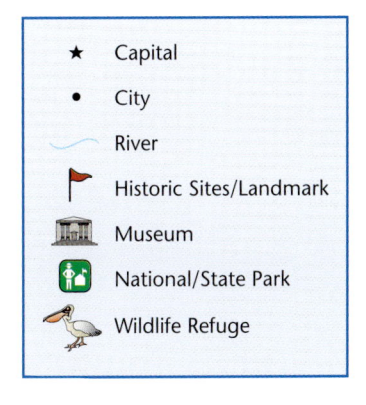

dinosaurs outside. The museum has a complete **triceratops** skeleton on display, and it has one of the most complete triceratops skulls ever found. Besides dinosaurs, the museum displays other types of fossils, rocks, and minerals from all over the world.

Bonanza Farms

Bonanza farming started when investors began to worry about the Northern Pacific railroad going bankrupt. The Northern Pacific received billions of acres of land from the government, and to raise more money to continue building the railroad west, they allowed shareholders to buy large tracts of land at a cheap price. Some stockholders bought many thousands of acres. Farms this large were called **bonanza farms.**

The Bagg Bonanza farm started this way. In the 1880s J.F. Downing, a Pennsylvania attorney, bought 9,000 acres of land near Fargo from the Northern Pacific Railroad. In 1886 Downing hired his nephew, F.A. Bagg, as a carpenter and field hand for $20 a month and free room and board. A year later he became superintendent of the ranch.

When Downing died, Bagg inherited 25 percent of the farm. A few years later, he moved the buildings and machinery from the farm to the land he inherited and began his own bonanza farm. The Bagg Bonanza Farm is the last restorable bonanza farm in the United States.

St. John's Church was built in nearby Horace. It was later moved to Bonanzaville, where it still holds church services and hosts weddings.

Bonanzaville, USA

Bonanzaville, a restored pioneer village, celebrates the history of North Dakota. The self-contained city features 40 museums from the past 150 years. The city has cowboy displays, pioneer displays, and farming displays.

The Big Hidatsa Village Site is on the National Register of Historic Places.

BIG HIDATSA VILLAGE SITE

A part of the Knife River Indian Villages Historic Site, this site commemorates the largest Hidatsa village, located near present-day Stanton. The Hidatsa grew squash, pumpkins, beans, sunflowers, and corn. They traded with other Native American peoples and made weapons to hunt the buffalo. The ruins, the displays of **artifacts,** and the reconstructed buildings give an idea of how the Hidatsa lived.

HUFF ARCHAEOLOGICAL SITE

The Huff Archaeological Site contains a **fortified** village on the Missouri River. The Mandan lived in the village during the 1400s. The village was made up of rows of houses with a large, ceremonial lodge near its center. The discovery of the village has provided information on how the early Mandan lived. It is the best-preserved site of the Mandan people and is on the National Register of Historic Places.

Built by the American Fur Company in 1828, Fort Union became a National Historic Site in 1966.

Fort Union Trading Post

From 1828 until 1867 the Fort Union Trading Post, located near Williston, was one of the busiest trading posts in the west. Native Americans traded tens of thousands of beaver pelts and buffalo hides each year. In the 1850s the fort shipped 150,000 buffalo robes out each year.

The fort was built near the present-day North Dakota-Montana border, where the Missouri and Yellowstone rivers join. Many Native American tribes, including the Arkikira, Mandan, Hidatsa, Cree, Chippewa, Blackfoot, and Lakota, came to the fort to trade.

In 1837 smallpox infected many Native Americans who visited Fort Union. The Native Americans carried the disease back to their tribes. Between 60,000 and 150,000 Native Americans died, including 90 percent of the Mandan and Hidatsa. The fort commanders tried to give medicine to the Native Americans, but they would not take it because they no longer trusted the commanders.

The fur trade continued until near the 1860s. At this time, the buffalo shifted **migratory** patterns, and so did the Native Americans that followed them. The fur company sold the fort to the army, who came to force Native Americans on to reservations. Because Fort Union was old, the troops tore it down and used the lumber to help build a new fort.

The International Peace Garden was dedicated in 1932.

INTERNATIONAL PEACE GARDEN

Located near Dunseith, the International Peace Garden covers 2,300 acres on both sides of the U.S.-Canadian border. More than 150,000 types of flowers bloom in the garden, which commemorates more than 150 years of peace between the two nations.

The International Peace Garden also includes a 100-foot tall peace tower, a bell tower, and a peace chapel. Inside the peace chapel engraved quotes by people of peace cover limestone walls.

The McHenry Railroad and Loop Museum

When trains first headed west in the United States, there was no way to turn them around, so railroads built giant loops. The loop was a big half-circle that made the train turn directions.

The McHenry Railroad Loop is the only remaining loop in the United States, covering 22 acres of land. To be more efficient, railways tore the loops down and built turntables, a turning metal circle on which a train engine can be parked. When the engine needs to go the other way, the turntable turns half-way around and the engine drives back on the tracks.

The McHenry Railroad Loop and its train station were built in 1899.

Map of North Dakota

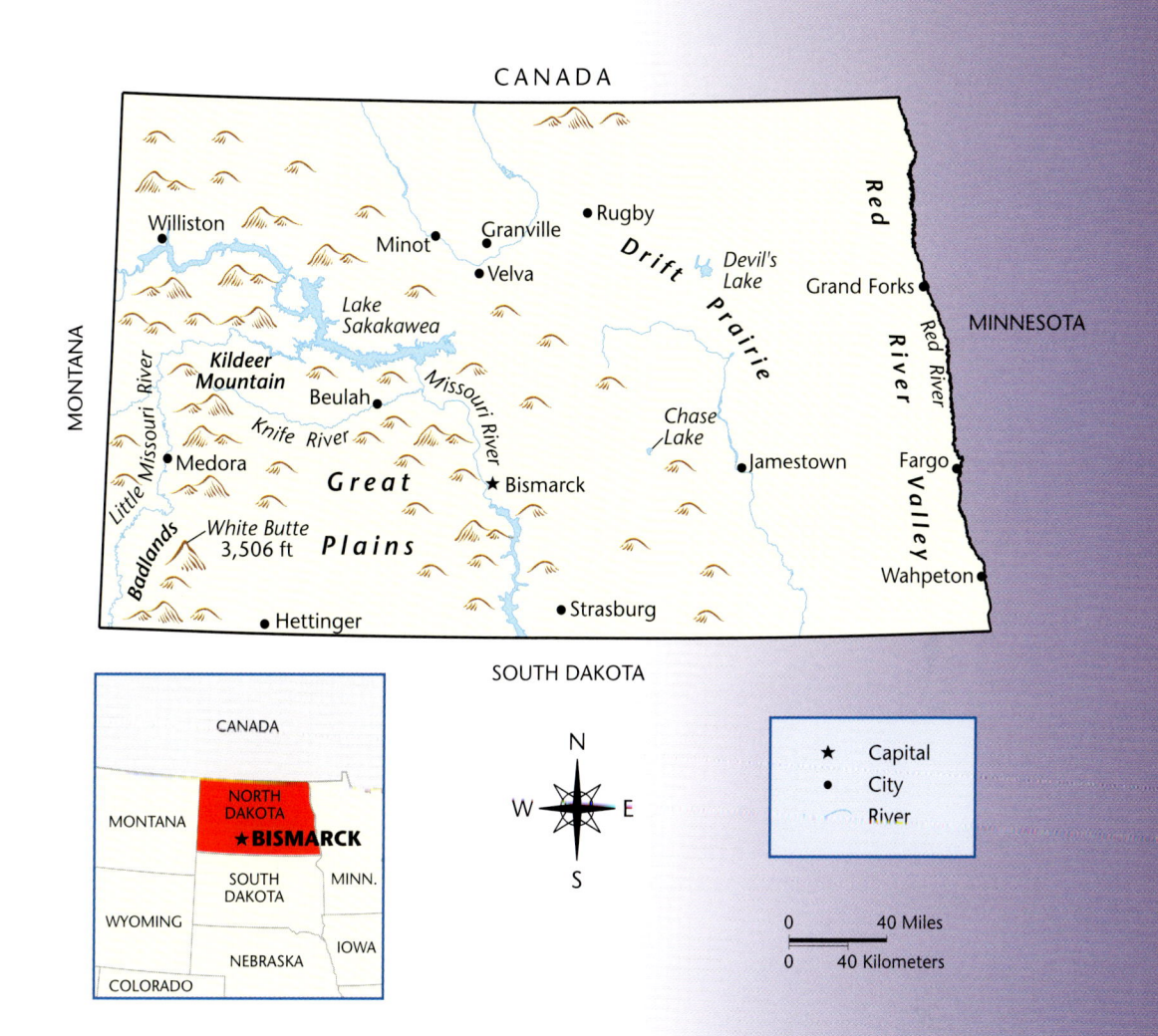

Glossary

albino person or animal born without normal pigmentation, producing white skin or hair and pink eyes

artifacts objects or tools made by humans

barter to exchange goods or services without using money

bonanza farms large, mechanized farms of the late 1800s located in the upper Midwest

butte steep hill with flat top

chemotherapy a treatment for cancer that uses chemicals

Chinook winds warm dry winds that swoop down the eastern side of the Rocky Mountains

civil case dealing with a person's private rights

climate the typical weather conditions over a period of many years

criminal case dealing with a crime committed

earth lodges Native American dwellings made from soil

flyway the path of migratory birds

fortified strengthened

glaciers thick, slow-moving sheets of ice that wear away the soil as they move

Grammy Awards annual music award presentations

integration the act of combining groups of people

jurist a judge

lefse a type of thin potato bread

legislature group of elected officials who make laws

lignite coal a brownish-black coal

lutefisk a Scandinavian specialty of air-dried codfish, which is soaked in water and lye before cooking

migratory relating to the movement of animals as they move from place to place

native local; belonging to the local area

nonpartisan an election in which the candidates do not belong to political parties

obelisk a four-sided pillar

organic farming farming without chemicals

petrified turned to stone

plains flat land surfaces

pop art movement a type of art in which common objects are used

powwow a Native American ceremony

refuges places of safety

rock johnnies piles of rocks which, according to legend, were piled up by sheepherders

Roosevelt, Theodore (1858–1919) 26th President of the United States, elected to two terms

silt rich soil that is left behind by a river or a stream

slough a place of deep mud

Spanish–American War a war between the United States and Spain, fought in 1898 over Cuba's struggle for independence from Spain

synthetic human made, rather than occurring naturally

triceratops a large plant-eating dinosaur with three horns and a bony crest

wetlands land areas that are swampy

World War II the war (1939–1945) between the Allies (Great Britain, France, Russia, the United States) and the Axis (Germany, Italy, Japan)

More Books to Read

Bruchac, Joseph. *Sacajawea: The Story of Bird Woman and the Lewis and Clark Expedition*. New York: Scholastic Paperbacks, 2001.

Fontes, Justine. *North Dakota: The Peace Garden State*. Milwaukee, WI: World Almanac, 2003.

Glasser, Rebecca Stromstad. *North Dakota*. Mankato, MN: Capstone Press, 2003.

Marcovitz, Hal. *Theodore Roosevelt*. Broomall, PA: Mason Crest Publishers, 2002.

Verba, Joan Marie. *North Dakota*. Minneapolis, MN: Lerner Publishing Group, 2002.

Index

agriculture, 6–7, 18, 30, 36–37
American elm, 13

Badlands, 19, 23–24
Bagg Bonanza Farm, 40
Bank of North Dakota, 10
beef, 30
Berwald, Lance, 35
Bismarck, 5, 10, 18, 29
bison, 9, 16, 19, 42
bonanza farms, 18, 39–40
Bonanzaville, 40

Carlsen, Anne, 21–22
Chase Lake, 10
Chinook winds, 8
climate, 7–8
courts, 27
Cowboy Poetry Gathering, 28
culture, 28–29

Dakota Bread (recipe), 31
Dakota Dinosaur Museum, 39
Dakota Gasification Company, 9
Davies, Ronald N., 20
Dmitre, Ivan, 19
Drift Prairie, 6, 7

Erdrich, Louise, 22

Fargo, 4, 8, 18, 20
"The Flickertail March", 15
folklore, 32–33
Fort Union Trading Post, 42
Frontier Village, 9
fur trade, 17, 42

geography, 6–7
glaciers, 6–7
government, 25–27
    executive branch, 27
    judicial branch, 27
    legislative branch, 26
Grand Forks, 5
Granville, 8
Great Northern Railroad, 4
Great Plains, 6, 7

Hettinger, 10
Hidatsa, 17, 41, 42
history, 16–19
Huff Archeological Site, 41

International Peace Garden, 12, 43

Jackson, Phil D., 22
Jacobsen, Dr. Leon O., 21
Jamestown, 9

Knife River Indian Village Historic Site, 41

Lakota, 4, 14, 16, 17, 32, 42
L'Amour, Louis, 21
Lewis and Clark Expedition, 17
lignite coal, 7, 9, 23–24, 37
Little Missouri River, 24
Louisiana Purchase, 17

Mandan, 16, 38, 41, 42
Maris, Roger, 22
McHenry Railroad Loop, 44
Menoken Village, 38
Minot, 29
Minot Air Force Base, 4, 36, 37

Native American Wars, 18–19
Native Americans, 4, 11, 16, 17, 29, 32, 38–39, 41, 42
natural gas, 9
Nokota horse, 14
Norsk Hostfest, 29
North Dakota Fighting Sioux, 34
"North Dakota Hymn" (song), 12, 13
North Dakota State Bison, 35
North Dakota State Fair, 29
North Dakota State University, 10, 35
Northern Pacific Railroad, 18, 40
northern pike, 13–14

Oimoen, Casper, 20
organic farming, 37

powwow, 28

railroads, 4, 5, 18, 40, 44
Red River, 5
Red River Valley, 6–7
refuges, 10
Roosevelt, Theodore, 12, 24
Roughrider State, 12
Rugby, 9

Sacajawea, 18
Severeid, Eric, 21
sheep, 10, 33
sports, 34–35
square dance, 15
state symbols
    bird, 13
    dance, 15
    equine, 14
    fish, 14
    flag, 11
    flower, 13
    fossil, 14
    grass, 15
    march, 15
    motto, 11–12
    nickname, 12
    seal, 11
    song, 12–13
    tree, 13

Teredo, 14
Theodore Roosevelt National Park, 24
Thompson, Edward K., 20–21
Thompson, Era Bell, 20

University of North Dakota, 20, 34

Ward, Dr. Joseph, 11–12
Welk, Lawrence, 20
Wells-Fargo Express Company, 4
western meadowlark, 13
western wheatgrass, 15
White Butte, 7, 33
White Cloud, 9
wild prairie rose, 13
wildlife, 7, 10
Writing Rock State Historic Site, 39

About the Authors

Jim Redmond lives in St. Peter, Minnesota, with his wife and two sons. He and his wife have visited the Badlands many times.

D. J. Ross is a writer with more than 25 years of experience in education. He has traveled throughout the United States and now lives in the Midwest with his three basset hounds.